CATACOMBS OF THE HEART

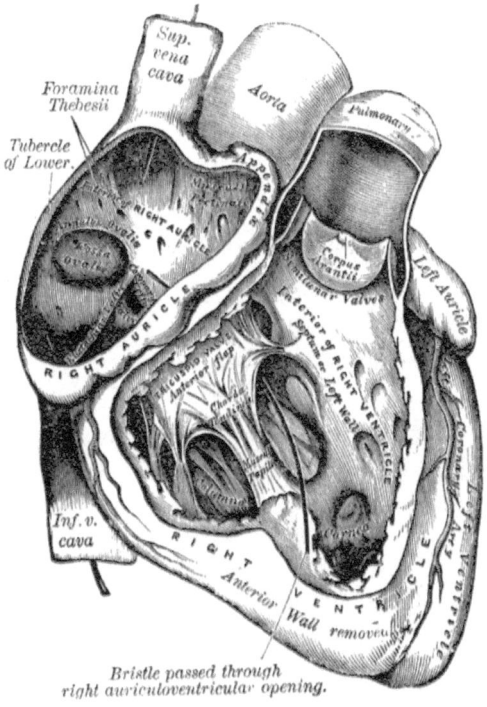

Poems by Mathieu Cailler

Luchador Press
Big Tuna, TX

Copyright (c) Mathieu Cailler, 2020
First Edition 1 3 5 7 9 10 8 6 4 2
ISBN: 978-1-950380-79-4
LCCN: 2019955707

Design, edits and layout: El Dopa
Cover image: Dirk Wenzel
Author photos: Kevin Grosher, Michael Collins
All rights reserved. No part of this publication may be reproduced or transmitted in any form or by any means, electronic or mechanical, including photocopying, recording or by info retrieval system, without prior written permission from the author.

Acknowledgments:

The author wishes to thank the following publications where these poems first appeared, some in slightly different form:

Words Dance: "Maybe Heaven's a Mulligan," "Somewhere on Hollywood Boulevard" and "My Mother Is the Statue of Liberty."
Forth: "Things That Trouble Me," "The Cadillac Lounge" and "Jesus's Yelp Review of Panda Express."

Like most books, there is only one author, but truth is every published work is a team effort, and I would thank these people that help, inspire, and keep my overall happiness index strong: Racquel Henry, Maggie Morris, my Vermont crew, Tim Antonides, Kali VanBaale, Courtney Ford, Donald Quist, Jennifer Cohen, Sophfronia Scott, Christina Gustin, Christiana Ward, Cheryl Wright-Watkins, Kevin Grosher, Adam Walch, Chaz Cipolla, Kim Holdsworth, Cris Boggiano, my South Carolina family, Tim Johnston, Cassie Ciopryna, Elizabeth Schmuhl, Zara Lisbon, Sue William Silverman, and Jason Ryberg, editor, publisher, and believer in my work.

And, of course, thank you to you, dear reader.

TABLE OF CONTENTS

Maybe Heaven's a Mulligan / 1
Somewhere on Hollywood Boulevard / 2
6:33 A.M. / 3
Grandpa's Thoughts After Two Old Crows
   and a Bad Bowl of Chowder / 4
My Mother Is the Statue of Liberty / 6
Cosmic Dust / 8
If I Were to Die Unexpectedly, Please Delete
   My Google Search History / 9
Cannolis and Whole Milk / 12
Prom Night / 13
Things That Trouble Me: / 14
Layaway / 16
Voicemail Left by a Friend of Mine / 17
Room 21 / 18
The Oral Tradition / 20
The Watched Inbox / 22
Absolution / 24
Flying into LAX / 25
Back in Time / 27
Globe / 29
Saturday Night in 1960s Harlem / 31
Deep into January / 34
Carbonara / 35
From a Letter Found in a Garage Sale Copy
   of The Sun Also Rises / 37

The Cadillac Lounge / 39

Sixers vs. Lakers on a December Night in 1995 / 42

Ring / 43

any & everything / 45

Window Shopping / 46

Someone Asked What I Dreamed About Last Night, but I
   Couldn't Tell Them This: / 47

The Day My Brother Died / 48

Bed's-Eye View / 50

Tijuana Music / 51

Mushrooms Grow on My Father's Tombstone / 52

dear ____: / 54

A Poem for Pablo Neruda / 55

Six-Feet Under / 56

Opposites Attract / 58

Jay Gatsby / 60

The Night of Conception / 61

Fetal Position / 62

Nothing to See Here / 63

Never a Mistake / 64

Every Now and Then / 66

Thank You / 67

Hell / 68

Meaning / 70

The Tragedy of Appreciation / 71

(Some) Things I've Gone Through / 72

No Matter / 73

Watching Bob Ross with Grandma on
   a Saturday Morning / 74

My Dog / 75

The Weight of a Soul / 76

Emojis Are Ruining the World / 77

Permanence / 78

Love Is the Loch Ness Monster / 79

This Password / 81

To the Little Girl / 83

Where Serotonin Flows Like Saturated Fat / 84

In Summer / 86

If You Must Know / 88

Obits / 89

New Nikes / 90

The Wondrous Names of Roses / 91

i carry your heart with me by e.e. cummings
   (without words) / 93

The Attic / 94

Permanent / 95

Jesus's Yelp Review of Panda Express / 97

Passing Tongues / 100

A Bistro & Baudelaire / 108

Dear Jesus / 110

Tired, but Beautifully So / 112

A Giraffe's Heart / 114

For Neebs, Big Al, & Sweet Lou

I want to write, but more than that, I want to bring out all kinds of things that lie buried deep in my heart.

-Anne Frank

I have felt that much of our poetry has been aimed at the heads of highbrows, rather than at the hearts of the people.

-Langston Hughes

Normality is a paved road: It is comfortable to walk, but no flowers grow on it.

-Vincent van Gogh

Maybe Heaven's a Mulligan

Here's how it might go down in my Nirvana,
Not Cobain's, not Siddhartha's, nor any other deities'.
Right there, on Interstate 89, I'd find you again at the
Tipsy Fox, making half circles on the rotating
bar stool, a sweating tequila in your grip. I'd puff
the same joke as last time, the one about Bon Jovi
that made your lips bend hard & your head brush back.
After a few drinks, I'd slam a song on the jukebox,
(E7 probably), & we'd dance again, humid, eyes holding,
shuffling our shoes on the puzzle-piece floor. This time, though,
I'd invite you back to my room, listen to your heels on the
walkway, the neon buzz of the Vacancy sign, & savor the
bolt of the door as it found its jamb. Then, there on the bed
of Room 18, I'd spelunkle your thighs, weld my hands
to your curves, & drop my mouth to your lips,
which I've always imagined

                                            taste like Friday.

Somewhere on Hollywood Boulevard

Today, on Hollywood Boulevard, near the Rob Lowe
star on the Walk of Fame, I passed a sitting bum
who wore cargo pants and a World's Greatest Dad
T-shirt. His feet were bare, grimy, and he was eating
an orange like an apple—gnawing right through the rind.
A copy of *Les Misérables* lay next to him, its pages fat and
swollen, and when a breeze pushed through, the sheets
ruffled, a pleasant sound, like leaves in the wind. I said,
Hello, and the man said, Hey—what's up, muchacho?
I reached for my wallet. I only had a five spot, but
since I'd already cracked the leather, I had to give him
something. Lincoln, he said. No shit. Good prez.
Better beard. Hell, sometimes I wish I'd gotten shot
in the theater. Nice way to go out if you ask me—
just bam, right there, while watching *Bye Bye Birdie*.
True, I said, before walking off. Wanna sit down?
he asked. I got some orange left, he said, and this
book here, that's depressing as shit. Fucking French
guys, right? Hard to get through even five pages
without tearing up a bit. What do you say?
Uh. Sure. Okay, I said. So I leaned up against a building,
lit a smoke, and listened to him as he cleared his
throat and started in. He had a pleasant reading voice,
especially applied to performing dialogue,
so I closed my eyes as his words blended
with the shuffle of passersby, the rumble of engines,
and the day-to-day buzz of honks and hollers.

6:33 A.M.

shaving soap,
a lather,
crumbs of sleep in eyes,
a yawn,
a dog walk,
the drip of hot coffee,

mascara, hairdryer heat,
shower steam,
newspaper ink,
bus-stop lines,
brown-bag lunches,
backpack zips,
hurry, gotta go,
see ya, love
you, me too,
bye bye,
call you later—

the thawing of day

these gradations of morning

Grandpa's Thoughts After Two Old Crows and a Bad Bowl of Chowder

Peanut allergies weed the herd
Thank you for coming means *good-bye*
Always try to park in the shade—shade is cheap, paint isn't
I'll call you means *you won't*
Hunger is the best sauce
Practice changing a spare two times a year because it will
    happen—and it will happen on a date
You're so sweet really means *you're pretty ugly*
Smacking a TV doesn't fix anything except frustration—and
    that's underrated
Nothing wrong with instant coffee
Only three ice cubes in your whiskey—more than that and it's
    a goddamn pop
See you round is *see you never*
Judge a racehorse by the size of its ass
You wanna be mysterious with women—talk less, nod more,
    pay with cash
Don't be a stranger is basically someone telling you that you
    need to hide better
Affection, smoke, and coughs are hard to hide
If you want to know how old a kid is, ask their grade level,
    then add five
Take good care is a nice way of saying *go fuck yourself*
Lie all you want, but don't do it to a lawyer, a doctor, or a wife
Make the same wish—birthdays, tunnels, shooting stars—
    God's got enough to remember

Love is nothing but delayed heartache
Never be rich enough to own a boat, just rich enough to
    have a friend who owns a boat
If you play she-loves-me/she-loves-me-not, be sure to
    grab a flower
with an odd number of petals

My Mother Is the Statue of Liberty
for Kali

Dragging her body out of the Buick,
grocery bags cradled in her arms,
eyeshadow matching the half circles
under her eyes, she shuffles to the front
door, wedges it ajar with her foot. Her
apron covered in coffee, mustard, some
sloppy joe sauce (the blue-plate special
on Thursdays at the diner). Setting her
purse down, she shuts her eyes, grabs
what she can of blackness, then asks
about my day, asks my brother the same,
asks about our spelling and math tests, then
asks Dad about his truck and if he was
able to find work at the Hy-Vee on I-80.
With one hand, she works off her apron,
mutters in a whisper that she can't believe
she wore it home, then funny enough, puts
it aside as she prepares a dinner of elbow
noodles and ground beef. No one asks
how her day was, and even if we did, she
would smile and say, *Good. Why don't
you get washed up… you finish homework?
Want to read together later? Checked
out a book at the small branch.* Her back
hunched, she starts the burner, and I
already know the rest of her hour: get

supper ready, set the table, carry out
the dish in red oven mitts, call for us to
get to the table—give me your tired,
your poor, your huddled masses—before
setting the casserole down and holding
out her hands to say grace.

Cosmic Dust
for Racquel

In the Milky Way and
other galaxies

stars live lives
not unlike us humans

burning out from
their cores, feeding
the sky their light, they
dim daily, see their
life expectancy wane
with each passing day

some fade, others explode,
and none, in all the billions,
are able to elude
their own mortality

If I Were to Die Unexpectedly, Please Delete My Google Search History

How do I know if a pineapple is ripe
How hard is it to count cards
How many stars are on the Walk of Fame
How many stars are there in the sky
How long do stars live
Where do I buy seaweed for sushi
Who in the hell published Mein Kampf
Who pierced Shakespeare's ear
Why did Shakespeare have a pierced ear
How do you pronounce hors d'oeuvres
Is it bad that I haven't seen Star Wars
Is Hans Solo in Star Wars or Star Trek
Does sour cream go bad
How much longer does OJ have to serve
Best place to buy a pug
How long do pugs live
Ways to tell a mango is ripe
Is Billie Jean King still alive
Best place in LA for a donut
How do I get a six pack
How do I grow my own weed
Why is my dog's stomach black
Why is my tongue black
Can weed make your tongue black
Can Pepto-Bismol make your tongue black

Why is my girlfriend pissed with me
When is Mother's Day
Why is my mother pissed with me
When is Father's Day
Why do men have nipples
Why is my tortoise swimming upside down
What happens when you swallow gum
How do I get rid of Internet Explorer
Where does Danny DeVito live
Does whiskey have medical benefits
Can you wear cowboy boots with a suit
What do I wear to an invite that says garden casual
What are The Golden Girls lyrics
If her pupils dilate does that mean she likes me
What does tergiversate mean
How do you tie a bowtie
How do you make tamales
Where do you buy good tamales
Are Geminis and Capricorns a good fit
Where is prostitution legal
How expensive is a prostitute
How expensive is a Vegas prostitute
Is God real
Is God out there
Does God hear me
Does God love me
Does he hate me
How can I get him to hear me

Are you God
Are you his middleman
Can you reach out to him
Can you tell him to listen to me
Can you talk to him
And, when you do, can you not mention the prostitute thing

Cannolis and Whole Milk

Cannolis and whole milk in
the pale flash of *The Tonight
Show*. Nana on the recliner,
her feet up, a fire to her side:
popping, struggling, embers
only now. A joke, laughter
on stage, in the audience, and
Nana's guffaw as well. Too
tired to move, too happy to sleep,
we loll in the cozy heat
of this mundane miracle.

Prom Night

A bowtie, a cummerbund, a hard-collared
shirt. Hand-wiping, mirror checkups, a
brushing of shoulders. The doorbell,
hellos, You look dapper, You look nice.
Want something to drink? Sparkling cider?
Coke? No I'm fine, Yeah me too, Okay, Okay,
What? Did you say something? Me? No.
Oh okay. A corsage, a *boutonniere*, a tango
of perfume and Bay Rum cologne. Photos flash
by the hearth, hands touch but do not
hold. Laughs pop but do not last. A smile,
a fidget, eye lashes so lashy. Dangling
earrings, cufflinks, a vest with buttons.
Dresses with satin, hair frozen with moose
and tortured into braids. Wallet inserted,
door opened. Knocks escape from heels
and wingtips. Waves, parents nod, See you,
Have fun, Be back soon, By 11, Drive safe,
Not too much fun, more waves, Yes,
Okay; Okay, yes. A shuffle to the Buick,
keys bulging in tapered trousers, glances to-
and-fro'—this Saturday night, stepping out,
where everything fits and yet nothing fits
at all.

Things That Trouble Me:

Just a few things that trouble me: dentists, middle seats, men who wear flip-flops out to dinner, heights, lawyers with ponytails, funny pilots, people who say *I'm not racist but...*, Lucille Ball's face, cookies with raisins, folks who wear more than one scarf, patrons who say *surprise me* to the bartender, compression shorts, corgis, the phrase *bomb dot com*, foam at fancy restaurants, my uncle's toupee, zippers that aren't YKK, fake eyelashes, abandoned tire swings, cereal that alters the color of milk, turbulence, *we need to talk, don't be mad when I tell you this*, merging onto freeways, those who believe the Earth came with borders, morons in infomercials, folks who make a production out of tasting wine, news tickers at the bottom of screens, non-dairy creamer, motel bedspreads, *got a second, heads up,* FYI, ASAP, those who never ask a question, people who fart on planes, water bottles, flat sheets, friends you can't get rid of, hotel room coffee pots, that air-puff test at the eye doctor, craft beer, motorcycle riders who wear tennis shoes, cops who ride horses, the microwave telling me to *enjoy,* hangnails, mouth-breathers, hold music, forgetting my password, finding the beginning of a roll of tape, damaged goods (of all sorts), reply-all emails, waitresses with long nails, people who pee in the urinal next to you, *you forgot to assign homework,* drive-thru screaming, guys who call girls *chicks,* CVS long-ass receipts, those stuffed-

animal claw vending machines, celebrities that can't
believe they're getting photographed on the corner of
Hollywood and Vine, PEZ candies, couples who own
a dog and call themselves *mommy* and *daddy,*
inspirational quotes posted online by people living
on a friend's couch, fruit cake, naked dudes who stretch in
the steam room, plastic on razor blades, the thought of not
hearing *I love you* back, the thought of not being able
to impress you, the thought of not being able
to keep you, the thought of penning your eulogy.

Layaway

The day after Christmas
the Kmart layaway area
is mostly bare
though some items remain—

a Barbie, a set of die-cast
model cars (one '56 Ford pickup,
one Porsche convertible), a
42L pinstriped blazer, a pair
of high heels, a Mickey Mouse
watch, a coffee pot, and a pair
of clip-on pearl earrings

and so the worker wipes
sleep from his eyes, hard
as breadcrumbs, and begins
loading the forgotten gifts
into a cart and making his way
down each fluorescent-lit aisle,
bringing his hand to each good
and each good to shelf

orphans, only dollars short,
from the certainty of family
and Christmas feasts

Voicemail Left by a Friend of Mine

Hey, man, today I finally drove my '87 Dodge Ram
to the moon.

No, no... no Cape Canaveral, no 3... 2... 1...
no exosphere or thermosphere or mesosphere...
gravity still very present, you know,
bringing me down.

No space suit either, made it in jeans
and a flannel. And I didn't even get there in one shot.
(My granddad completed about half the voyage
before he passed and gave me the truck.)

But I did make it to the moon, kind of.
Today the quarter ton's odometer rolled
to 250,000 miles—the distance from the
Earth to the moon.

I didn't plant a flag, or throw my arms up,
or say *giant step for whatever.*

I pulled over to the side of I-96 and thought
about that view—that little blue marble with
all those countries and all those people and all that
chaos and confusion.

Shoot, pal, it's enough to make a man keep driving.

Room 21

Let's go back to the Econo Lodge
in Berlin (not Germany, but Vermont)
where, even in January, we sat on the
metal fire escape that overlooked
the frozen Winooski and people's
shoddy Xmas lights. Let's go back
to that room on the second floor
where the bedspread looked like
your Uncle Roy's holiday sweater, and
where the mini fridge churned 24/7 and
the faucet dripped to keep time. Let's go
back to that spot and smoke strong
weed rolled in Bible pages 'cause *someone*
(me) forgot to pick up the Zig Zag papers. Let's
tear the sheets out carefully, not only
for the perfect joint, but for the perfect meaning,
too. Let me pick the passage this time,
something from Corinthians, 13:4 maybe,
a little ditty like *Love is patient, love is kind.*
It does not envy, it does not boast.
It is not proud. It is not rude.
It keeps no record of wrongs.
I like that one. Well, especially that last
part—don't you?
Or maybe Romans 12:9
Love must be sincere. Hate
what is evil; cling to what is good.

Or Peter 4:8
Above all, love each
other deeply, because love covers over
a multitude of sins
Or maybe it's just one of those moments,
one of those days, when I've been reading the
Bible too much, searching for meaning,
'cause God's a default friend, and you're
long gone.

The Oral Tradition

we tell the children from the moment they're out of the
    womb and into the world
that they should believe in themselves
and Santa and the Easter Bunny, too

we tell the children that voting makes a difference,
superheroes are alive, and that the Tooth Fairy
will be by soon with a five spot for your
molar

we tell the children to believe in manners
and kindness
and that your self is
good enough

we tell the children to believe in angels
and happiness and hard work
as well

only

to little
by little

ween
the children of these hopes
and magic dust

until they awaken
one morning and find out
that love is divorce
and Kris Kringle
is Costco

and that the world
and its chimney flues
were never filled
with anything other
than soot and ash

The Watched Inbox

you told me right before
the semester was over
that you would email me

you told me this as we sat
in the cafeteria after I gave
you that snow globe
of Philadelphia with Rocky
and the Liberty Bell

before we trekked up to
your dorm room and
I helped you pack
and we took three trips from
room to Jeep

you gave me a kiss on
the lips and thanked
me for last night

said it was perfect

then you let the Jeep
heat up

plumes of smoke mixed
with the exhaust

and then you wrapped yourself
in another coat and I
opened the door and
you got in

and now, I am home, too
took the bus and already kissed
Mom and Dad

I already said goodnight to them

the living room is empty
except for Jimmy Fallon on the TV,
dancing and singing

and the computer on my lap, that warms
as I wait
for an email from you

and get teased every time the Inbox
goes bold and says 1

because it's not you

it's just diet tricks
and money scams
and so many
penis pills
that promise
the best promises

Absolution

through the confessional screen, i'm holy,
kind of

dear father, i have sinned. it has been one
month since my last confession: i did it
all really. ran the table. swearing, gluttony,
stealing, lust, sex, and speeding. even free
music and movies, too, from an online source
that gave my computer a trojan horse.

a deep breath from the priest. then a cough.
okay, my son, a little less than the previous
month, it seems. so that's better. 20 hail marys,
10 novenas, and 5 our fathers. heck, maybe you
should think about donating an organ, too,
he says. then laughs. then coughs.

i return home. and start on the prayers
once in the kitchen, but lose track soon enough
and then words jumble and pile up, and i take a
break. make my own holy trinity: one with bitters,
bourbon, and sweet vermouth.

Flying into LAX

At 22,000 feet, the foreplay of your
being begins to gleam: strips
of lights, knots of freeways, cars
zooming on concrete strips like
platelets through corroded arteries;
beaches' waves consistent, pounding;
a heartbeat, a jazz drum—pushing on
through riots and lootings, fires and
mudslides, weddings, divorces, sweet
nothings and barbs.

Through the plane's
windows, people trace their fingers
down your roads—the 10, the 210;
the 405 and the 91.

They close one eye,
get their fingers out, pretend
they're giants: squish the US Bank tower,
pluck the point of the Capitol Records building,
and squeeze the letters of the Hollywood sign.

You're disconnected, not New York,
smoggy, ugly, your traffic
is shit

And what do you do?—

just continue to bring the sun,
watch the population swell,
and keep auditioning

for a role
that was always yours.

Back in Time

Today, on a summer day, she decides
to time travel without flux capacitors
or Doc Brown or the need of an 88 mph
DeLorean. Just her, her pug (Isabelle),
and her Volkswagen Eurovan. Heading
south—dunes to her left, ocean on the right—
she arrives at her high school that she
thinks is aging better than Rob Lowe.
The red-tile roof flickers with late sun,
and the same palms thrash with sea
wind. She strolls the outdoor halls,
certain that her 8½ size flat is stepping
into footprints of old when she wore
overalls and a low-slung JanSport and
flannels to be like Nirvana even though
it was SoCal, and it was 93 degrees in
September. She wanders the perimeter,
sips from the drinking fountain that
still has zero pressure, and makes her
way toward the baseball dugout where the
old pine still bowers the field. *Tattoo it*, she
remembers him saying. And she recalls
his left-cheek dimple and the screwdriver
he'd stolen from the custodian's shed.
Here, take it, he'd added. And she'd

gone to work, carving *RC loves CB*
into the soft bark of the tree that
continues to photosynthesize,
and spread its roots and limbs not
unlike, she thinks, the actual people
who still bear the initials.

Globe

Maybe my brain isn't a series of nerves
and pink-gooey folds, but a map, a globe—
spinning with swaths of continents,
countries, and cities I can't pronounce.
Masses of land that remind me of you—
Russia, cold and foreign, chugging trains
over tundra, cold breath of the world
smacking the iron of the eastward pushing
locomotive. France, a fleck of time that is
no longer spoken of—backpacking, hostels,
dipping our hot legs in Lourdes.
One-night stands, benders, cigarettes rolled
with Bible pages—archipelagos of warmth,
swollen with salty water; distant like
Turks and Caicos; curves and points; broken
shards of earth. Sourness; hatred: small
in mileage, hard in fight—a Middle East
that prickles with abuse and injustice. Rage
that consumes me at any moment. Rushing
rivers of Montana, fly fishing, and rainbow
trout with skin speckled, iridescent, like motor
oil in puddles—are my holidays—Christmas,
Easter, Thanksgiving—when thoughts are
smooth, idle. But my Amazonian rainforests,
too, are being chopped down, razed, burned.
Apartheid present in my medulla oblongata—
the genocide of innocence—when days

of backpacks, baseball, bike rides, Easy-Bake
Ovens—now replaced by loans, marriage,
fast food, and stony silences. I, too, dream
of Hawaii in my globe, of Spain and bulls,
of Australian girls with tan lines on their shoulders
and dimples on their lower backs, sumo
matches outside of Nagasaki, safaris and
tribal dances, but I'm not sure I can afford
the ticket, take off work, for I'm stuck on a
boat outside of Oman. In time, though,
maybe it'll be possible to leave, maybe
catch a current, maybe a walk will bring me
tranquility, spin me to the spot in the
Kansas prairie, outside of Coffeyville, where
the wind sighs like clockwork, swirling tall
blades of wheat and rye.

Saturday Night in 1960s Harlem

I was 14 the first time I walked into a bar, wearing a thrift
    shop, Prince of Wales suit
There I met with two friends, who'd both brought girls
They were older and left me behind after two Fuzzy Navels
    and one Tom Collins
I finished up my beer and peeled the soft label from its skin
    and watched
a handsome man flirt with girls by the piano

Old-movie cool, in a black-and-white world, lighting girls'
    cigarettes with one hand
while the other ran through his hair
He wore a black T-shirt paired with charcoal slacks
I couldn't see his shoes because women were always
    standing in front
of him, throwing their heads back at his jokes

It would have made more sense to stare at the ladies,
    as it was the closest I'd ever been to any
magazine women—all the women I knew were old and
    Catholic, a throw-in with the
Louisiana Purchase—but I didn't gaze their way
I focused on the man, thinking I could learn something

Hours later, when a few of the girls fluttered away, the man
stood alone at the bar and ordered another bourbon with
    three ice cubes

And I noticed his shoes then: black and white, like a diner's floor
Hey, I said
And he looked right at me, like speaking to a 14-year-old
in a billowy suit on a Saturday night in Harlem
was routine
How can I help you? he said, whiskey working off his tongue

I unbuttoned my wool jacket and leaned his way
How do you do it? I asked
He stopped, took a drink, Do you know jazz, he said,
    Do you listen to jazz?
A little, I said, but…
Stop, that's it, listen to jazz, the man said
Just listen to jazz? I said, My uncle does that and women
    hate him, I said
He pulled a cigarette from his pocket and popped it
    between his lips,
a gold tooth at the back of his mouth glinted as he chuckled

I shouldn't have used the word listen, he said, it's more like
hear—you have to hear jazz… and not just a little either,
not just a song or two, but I want you to backstroke in it,
overdose on bebop, make it a part of you, don't just get it
stuck in your head, but try to get it to live in your body—see
it all as one big album: Zoot Sims, Mezz Mezzrow, Muggsy
Spanier, Max Roach, Bunny Berigan, Cab Calloway, Lockjaw
Davis. Learn their notes; dance their melodies; improv their
improvisations; hear enough of it to fill swimming pools with
quarter notes and rest symbols

Okay, I said, Is that what you were talking to those girls
about? Discussing jazz?

His cigarette had burned half-way through, but the ash
was intact. Women fluttered behind him—feathers to his
peacock. No, I never talk about jazz with girls, but you'll hear
it when you speak, when you get dressed, when you smile,
and it's hard to be an asshole when you're high on Brubeck
His large hand shook my small one, and I buttoned my jacket
and thanked him, smiled at one of the ladies over his right
shoulder.
She returned the favor, probably because I was in his aura

When I got outside, I found a cab with the light on and told
the driver to take me home,
and I asked him if he wouldn't mind putting on some jazz
88.4 okay? the driver asked
Uh, sure, I said, that's my favorite, perfect

We drove round the grid of the city, and I savored the sounds
while staring out the window at all the lights in all the tall
buildings, where no one was home

A coy piano, timid cymbals
At first I thought the volume was low, but then jazz flew out:
the trumpet awakened and a piano danced with it, twirled,
clutched the small of its back

I started to learn right there, in the back of the yellow Crown
Victoria; the world unfurled,
and the DJ came through some minutes later

That was Chet Baker, he said,
and that was Almost Blue

Deep into January

Now in the New Year
We've put the ex
in Xmas
Advent calendars'
doors ripped open;

all 24 chocolate tenants
evicted from their apartments

Christmas lights stripped from
eaves and trees—some blinking;
others burnt from
too much cheer

Pants tight, belt digging—
resolution already foregone

A dry pine strewn on the road,
a line of tinsel as a trail of blood,

and there, on the front lawn, a puddle
of a snowman (due to a warm front):
a newsboy cap, a pipe,
and a carrot

left as holiday spatter

Carbonara

they're off, doing what parents do
on Friday nights, so we are here
with grandma (grandpa was sent
to the hardware store to buy a new
snow shovel & some more matches)

wherever they are, they aren't as
comfortable as we are: wearing
clothes that were only designed
for these kinds of nights: sweats
that billow, chunky socks, & T-shirts
that wrap like soap

they are probably out to dinner
at some downtown restaurant where
their feet hurt in hard shoes & where
water is delivered to the table in
glass bottles

but they don't have grandma in the
kitchen, the Knicks on TV, or
the smell of pancetta in the air.

dinner will be ready soon, boys,
grandma says for the second time,

so we begin towards the table

she says something else, too, about
how spaghetti carbonara is an Italian
dish that is named after coal miners
because the pepper (which she won't
use because we hate it) looks
like coal dust

everything around me is hot: the
fireplace to the north, the kitchen
to the east, the heater to the west, &
the dryer spinning behind me

all this temperature, swarming,
trapped inside,

sealed in by storm windows

From a Letter Found in a Garage Sale Copy of *The Sun Also Rises*

Carol:

Today, at noon,
somewhere
along the Pacific,

where the parking
was easy and the
sandpipers plentiful,

I finally wrote you
that love letter.

I scrawled it right there,
in the wet sand,
with a sharp stick.

Five nice sentences,
all huddled in a box.

Then, I watched the
tide rise, and the
waves come in,
their salty bodies,
slithering,
licking all the
letters clean.

Before my words
had a chance to
breathe.

Before you even
had the chance
to read them.

The Cadillac Lounge

a Tuesday in early March
at a strip club off the
train tracks in Providence
      where
the neon is burned out
          so the sign
just reads, The Cad Lounge

it's advertised as a spot
         with the
most beautiful women
that *wear nothing more*
         than a
smile and a G-string

music thunders and men
         stay still
in leather-backed seats
         confusing
erections for affection

sweaty bills wadded in fists
shiny with grease
         from
chicken wings and curly fries

lust seethes through bloodshot

                        eyes and
half smiles

stamped-out Marlboros and
Camels, these bent worms
of addiction

bass rips and bodies
glide—a dance, a flash,
a clack
         of high heels

bodies lacquered with perfume
                and lotion
                and caked-on
makeup to camouflage
                black eyes

midriffs undulate like the
                winter Atlantic

and transactions follow—
legal tender for human
touch

the night passes
           like this

with no way to see time move
other than the

          wristwatch
of the bouncer
who cuts on the fluorescent
          tubes at 2 a.m.

allowing the dancers
to tuck behind
          the curtain
to the dressing room backstage
          hot
with naked light bulbs and mirrors

where they
remove their makeup
and persona, swapping
Cinnamon for *Cindy*

and wrap themselves
          in heavy winter garb

coats and boots and
          stocking caps

to ward off the many advances
          heaved
          by that
          Rhode Island chill

Sixers vs. Lakers on a December Night in 1995

they all went to bed an hour ago / sleeping down the hall / Dad with hard exhales and Mom with snorting inhales / my older brother, Tony, asleep above me, on the top bunk / I listen to the game on my Walkman / 570 AM and Chick Hearn's voice / the volume is low, and the sheets are up / rain falls on this December night, but not loud enough to disturb the game / in fact loud enough to muffle the sound of my headphones, so I hope the storm pushes harder / the Lakers were down by 14, but they are making a run / Van Exel has swished back-to-back threes and made it a game with nine minutes to go / pump fake, windmills, the ball is swatted into the third row / 17,000 fans explode / their cheers thunder / and I turn the volume down / the game is tight / a timeout / my heart beats like a second hand / with each dribble and sneaker squeak, I hold on to the words / dribble drive, no-look pass, up-and-under, he lays it in / I allow a scream into the pillow / a tie score with less than two minutes to go / one timeout left / hands clasped / ears alert / body rigid / all this anxiety wrapped / in flannel pajamas

Ring

It's time, she thinks,
Four months

The marriage has
Now been legally
Over for sixteen weeks

Morally over for more than
Two-and-a-half years

She has only taken
The ring off once before

In April of '95
After a golf accident,

A sprain,
A pinky and ring finger
Tweak

But now the house is calm
The sky cold and
Cloudless

And courage is strong
In this moment

Like freshly sprayed perfume

It's okay, she thinks

Rubbing some lotion on
Her single digit

Priming and spinning
Twisting and yanking

Before the thin, 18-karat band
begins to glide

Freeing skin that's been
Clutched for years,
Letting air access the epidermis

Allowing the flesh to
Fatten and fill the space

Once more

any & everything

jealous of the cashmere
that heats your
shoulders; of the flat sheet
that cocoons your body;
of the soap suds that
ride your calves; of the
summer tendrils that
bleach your hair; of the
bobby pins that fasten
your strands; of the wind
that wraps you with a
quick breath

of laughs; of spoons;
of clouds; of cigarettes

of grass; of cups;
of songs

of him, of him, of him

Window Shopping

I pass windows and bookstores
and think of all the gifts
I'd buy you:

dusty first editions,
pastel sketches,
even a brooch of a swan

(like you told me
your grandmother used to wear)

but you are not my girl,
and thus, these aren't my
purchases to make

so instead I keep
heaps of imaginary treasures
in my brain

and envision all
the imaginary
wrapping paper
you'll never shred

Someone Asked Me What I Dreamed About Last Night, but I Couldn't Tell Them This:

I wrote a poem about what it was
to be your left, front tooth

the lace in your bra,
the print of your palms,
the creases of your eyes,
the rivets on your jeans

I was the skin on the back
of your knees,
a papercut on your pointer finger,
your hemoglobin,
a taste bud on your savory side,
your frosty irises,
a freckle in the valley of your breasts

I was even your pinky toenail
in your morning shower,

covered with soap suds,

swirled in hot water

The Day My Brother Died

I ate refried beans for breakfast
The DOW closed up 14 points
CNN was rambling on about Ukraine
A neighbor's trees were being trimmed
My bathroom faucet started dripping
The blender I ordered from Amazon arrived
I returned a Netflix documentary on minimalism
I bought floss and sunglasses at CVS
Kobe scored 42 points
I got a parking ticket
The soup of the day at the diner was tomato bisque
My dog had an ear infection
I took 4 Advil
I prayed 19 times
I saw an old friend from high school
A girl I used to date texted me about getting together
I didn't dream
My watch started slowing down
A hangnail bothered me
The sunset was pinkish
Snow leopards were put on the endangered species list
A mudslide took out some of Malibu
There was a SIG alert on the 405 freeway
I didn't shampoo
My lips were dry
I missed an acupuncture appointment
Two cars honked at me

I wrote three emails
I washed the casserole dish
My boss got married
I wore black jeans and a blue T-shirt
Lasagna was being served in the hospital cafeteria
"Midnight Train to Georgia" played on the cab ride home
I received an Evite to my friend's Cinco de Mayo party
My college called and asked me for money
There was a bird roosting under my bedroom eave
There were 14 messages on my voicemail
There were girls playing double-dutch at the park
There was a 40 percent chance of rain

Bed's-Eye View

Woke up this morning and
saw you getting dressed in
front of the mirror.

The tug-of-war between
affection and sleep was strong,
but affection won out in the end.

I watched you slide and
wiggle into your jeans,
slip into your boots.

Would I ask for your number
again?

Keep the napkin
with the bleeding digits
in my wallet
for all these years?

Yes,
if I'd be so lucky.

Yes.

Tijuana Music

This song again: buses hissing, honking, children cackling,
a scream of engines huddled in close proximity,
crushed cilantro, lowered lids, "Agüita de Melón" leaking
from an old Buick speaker, emaciated dogs panting
on dusty streets, zebra-painted donkeys resting with
fly-covered eyes, gasoline sharpness, palm fronds sighing,
houses in colored-pencil hues, red-tiled roofs
reflecting UVs, helicopters pounding the sky,
street-corner tacos, crushed Tecates along the roadside,
flickers of Guadalupe candles, too;
rooster crows, Zona Norte's red lights, piles of peppers
at El Mercado Hidalgo, cuánto cuesta?, pesos clinking
between cracked palms, motorbikes buzzing, piñata fringe
stirring with wind, rusted pickups with no tailgates,
upside-down dead chickens in storefront windows,
heat on tongues, beaches with as many humans as sand
granules,
July flavor, T-shirts clinging to back sweat,
church bells thundering at Plaza Santa Cecilia,
hissing nostrils and red capes at El Toreo de Tijuana,
and theses
Pacific waves
    that are unable
    to differentiate
between U.S. and Mexican soil—
just pounding the coastline
with every flow and ebb,
finding the same taste, lick
                    after lick

Mushrooms Grow on My Father's Tombstone

Past the wrought-iron gates
and onto the dewy field,
lies my father and his tombstone,

marked simply
with his name (no middle initial)
and the date of his arrival and
departure,

nothing more
than a dash
to signify his work,
and lovers, and Mets watching,

his 7 & 7s, his retrievers, and his hearty
guffaws

Wild mushrooms sprout
around his headstone, some even
using the granite for support

Pale-yellow chanterelles, with fleshy
gills, and morels, too, comprised of
honeycomb helixes

Others' names evade
but they're white, with fragile
stems and tiny caps,

and these fungi are only
on his stone,

because I have,
once more,
forgotten flowers

dear ____:

make me
like you used to

as much
as you can

as best
as you can

without apologies
without fear

with freedom
with madness
with love

yours always,
-art

A Poem for Pablo Neruda

in my twenties, I visited Santiago
with the hope of touring your famous
home, La Chascona

but, when I arrived,
the line was long & packed
& as serpentine
as the Chilean coast,

so instead I opted to spend time
with a woman I'd met the
night prior

we strolled La Calle de Santa Julia,
shared hand-rolled cigarettes,
& exhaled plenty of
Spanish sweet nothings

I apologize, dear Pablo,
but you, of all people,
I'm sure
can understand

Six-Feet Under

Not all death is six-feet under; sometimes it's frozen weather
Leaves stripped, raw branches, birds' nests left to dwindle, decay

Sometimes it's a phone call unanswered, a text ignored
Words unfiltered, a postcard improperly addressed

Not all death wears black suits and throws dirt onto
    varnished caskets

Sometimes it's a job overseas, a promotion, a glance, a laugh
    when
A hug is needed

Sometimes it's a sloppy kiss, a detached gaze, a large bed
    with a cold
No-man's land of soft sheets between two bodies

Sometimes it's a fight, a lack of one

Sometimes it's a secret,
Many of them that eventually leak from a
Brain's corner

Sometimes it's a hotel room in Dallas and too much bourbon

Sometimes it's dressed up, disguised as fun, staring at you
From across the table with a glass of wine, bangs in her face,
Freckles on her bare shoulders

Sometimes it's a silent cab ride home, diapers unchanged,
Piles of egg-yolk dishes, the evening news, a decayed tire
    swing

Sometimes it's a thrift-shop teddy bear, an uncracked book on
    a nightstand,
An *Okay, okay,* an *I wish you the best,* a car that won't
    start at 2 a.m.

Sometimes it's an old flame that extinguishes a new one
Sometimes it sneaks
Sometimes it smiles

Sometimes it waves, nods,
Sometimes it's as simple as good-bye

Opposites Attract

You, at the bar, with the empty glass and full smile,
fake eyelashes and real boobs, high heels and low-cut
shirt:
    Maybe we can go out sometime
    or stay in
    Maybe hold hands and release pain
    Maybe we can live on this street where
    parking's a bitch, but the view's a winged
    angel
    Maybe I can cook for you with Whole Foods
    groceries while we empty bottles of wine
    Maybe we can live a life of Fridays even
    on Mondays, find hope in each other's
    hopelessness, feel our spirits lift even
    when our dreams feel sunk
    Maybe one day we can
    drink skinny margaritas while
    we play with our fat dog Hubert
    Maybe we can forget the past and remember
    that pizza place in Red Hook, drive
    your grandma's old Honda down some new
    roads, laugh at each other and cry when needed
    Maybe we can turn off the world and turn on
    some Bowie, some Brubeck
    Maybe I see too much in too little time
    Maybe that's my pain, my splendor
    Maybe we should live in the now and

pretend the future is later
>>Maybe we can spend time
getting lost
>>just to find ourselves
>>over—
and again

Jay Gatsby

Jay Gatsby had it easy

he knew where Daisy was
where she lived

he knew he could lure her with
music and champagne and black-tie affairs

But I cannot

For my Daisy
Is a petal in acres of roses

A single girl in LA County
One in millions

So I stand on the cliffs near the Pacific

And look for that green flashing light

Across miles of water and concrete

To stare at nothing
but smog

The Night of Conception

You two sojourned in Barcelona
Rented a Citroën
Blasted "Tiamo" by Umberto Tozzi on repeat
Drove too fast
Put all four windows down
Shared tapas at a small spot on La Rambla
Made sure the food didn't harm your grins
Laughed at the waiter with the poorly glued toupée
Smoked clove cigarettes
Smiled till your cheeks throbbed
Blew on your hands
Tightened your scarves
Wore uncomfortable shoes
Huddled your bodies
Flung coins into fountains
Wished for what you already had
Swapped stories
Gave money to a harmonica-playing street performer
Toasted to 1977
Shut your eyes when a gust blew strongly
Tilted your heads back at the slightest speck of humor
Strolled arm-in-arm
Eye-contacted hard enough to make fire
Bolted the door to Room 219
Said no to sleep
Said yes to each other

Fetal Position

one a.m.
        I lay in the fetal position
        in bed
knees up, a foam pillow
between my legs

I'm 34
        well past being conceived
        well past development

an adult, some might say

yet this infantile position
is always nourishing, always home

        never too old to be reborn
        to be more
                by morning

Nothing to See Here

Is there such a thing as a new poem?
Have they all been written?
Have we ever scrawled something fresh
since the painted horses and bulls of Lascaux?
Is this all just a retelling,
a soulful
regurgitation
of old campfire tales?
Stale have-I-told-yous,
Lost echoes of despair and splendor?

Never a Mistake

It's never a mistake
    to sleep in
    ask the girl to dance
    order the French fries
    make a child laugh
    pop champagne
    tell her how you feel
    buy an old motorcycle
    wear a tie
    speak the truth
    laugh with friends
    stop at a kids' lemonade stand
    cook pancakes
    pour another glass of wine
    study the moon
    listen to crickets
    pick flowers
    wish on dandelions
    build a fire
    drive a convertible at night
    go skinny dipping
    read all night in bed
    have another slice
        risk the sunburn
        forgive wholeheartedly
        leave too big a tip
        bake a rhubarb pie
        sing a lullaby
        savor the sunrise

soak in a train's whistle
trace the backroads
nap in the shade
bite into ripe figs
    stand in a downpour
    drag your finger across constellations
    say I miss you
    tuck a strand of hair behind her ear
    interlock fingers
        or to take the trip
        to Paris

Every Now and Then

you wish you could die

just so you could hear

the eulogy

that might

just keep you living

Thank You

thank you for
passing through me
like a breeze
through a windchime

Hell

I'm not so sure that hell exists
but I do know
that it must be like
    a Day's Inn in Tampa
    a Sunday at Costco
    Black Friday at Best Buy
    the comments section on YouTube
    a nine-hour layover in Atlanta
    New York subways in August
    a Del Taco bathroom stall
    the quiet of a widow's home
    a children's hospital
    dusty attic toys
    driving away from the vet's with just a leash
    an EBT card being declined
    a little girl in high heels for the first time
    a kid's balloon slipping from his grip
    election ads
    an abandoned tire swing on an unkempt limb
    the *Santa* talk
    the erosion of a glacier
    week-old roadkill
    the permanence of the past
    the brightness of a hospital room
    people who don't know their worth
    hashtags
    Christmas trees on the 26th

the 11 o'clock news
training bras
the last page of a perfect book
airport good-byes
the trashcan after Thanksgiving
the flash of an AR-16
a crop-duster's chemicals
migrants who want nothing more than safety
an Ethiopian boy's sharp, exposed ribs

Meaning

there are moments—thousands even—
that I've yet to understand
but my skills seem to be sharpening

while many of us attempt to dissect
the meaning of life—and pile on work
as its definition

I've come to understand it differently,
especially here with you

on this Sunday morning, the cat stretched out,
twisting in a spot of late-spring sun, you with
your glasses on, the Times quartered, and a pencil
between your fingers in anticipation of a crossword
eureka!

there's a Dolly Parton record spinning, the smell
of pancakes on the griddle, their bubbles sprouting
before the flip,

and thick peace
that I want to hold tenderly
and press against my chest
as if it were a newborn

The Tragedy of Appreciation

sometimes I can't help
but wonder
about all the insects
I've crushed
while walking around
and savoring nature

(Some) Things I've Gone Through

239 jars of jelly
432 cans of tuna
9 homes
18 swimsuits
14 roommates
4,112 rolls of toilet paper
12 barbeques
5 basketball nets
3,143 bars of soap (mostly Dove)
16 phones
22 computers
17 couches
5 wheelbarrows
14 TVs
118 pairs of sneakers
6,229 bottles of beer (not on the wall)
4 classic cars
13 dogs
1,336 books (mostly read)
3 hamsters
2 cats
6 record players
14 baptisms
33 funerals
12 girlfriends
2 wives
1 heart

No Matter

no matter how hard we try,
we are all the grotesque

all of us
the unwanted:

nocturnal raccoons with sharp clams and curved spines,
hissing across the dumps of outer New Jersey

we are all bloated New York rats, chewing hot garbage,
fucking behind drywall, or shiny roaches
clustered in the feces of septic tanks,
skittering under linoleum tiles as soon as the lights cut on

and everyone is out, setting traps
and blasting chemical sprays, and screaming,
Ew! Shoo! Get! Get!

Watching Bob Ross with Grandma on a Saturday Morning

Grandma lays out newspaper on the dining-room table

and then pulls out the supplies she bought:

two canvases, oil paints, brushes, and she angles the TV

so we can see it better

   And we start applying specks of color,

     listening to the curly-haired man who looks like

     he's never been sad

     happy trees, he says, rays of sun, he says, make

        everything matter, he says

          And I follow his instructions, look at

            Grandma's smile and hands,

              and it's the first time in my life that I know

                I'll miss a moment even though I'm currently living it

My Dog

the sun cascades
through the den's window,
lighting up a square
of the floor in Broadway fashion
in which the poodle rests
on his side and snores,
only awakening every hour or two
to follow the lit-up, warm wood—
something of a curly sundial
in this complicated world

The Weight of a Soul

never worry about being too much
for some people—some are just
too weak to bench press your soul

Emojis Are Ruining the World

I worry that the more we use
happy faces, eggplants, balloons,
and thumbs-ups

the more we revert back to hieroglyphics

the more we pass on articulating sentiment
press pictures instead of swirling in their meaning

the more emojis pepper our prose
the more we use different colored hearts
the more our real ones,
all four chambers of them,
begin to atrophy

Permanence

In September of 1963, a bomb blast
killed four girls at a church here
on Sixteenth Street in Birmingham, Alabama

And even though passersby carry groceries
and smile and barbershop poles spin and it's
73 degrees and sunny and thick clouds
stretch overhead

And yes, it's been decades, and the street
now smells of sticky buns and hardware stores,
not sulfur and fire, and sure, the parishioners
weren't my relatives, and I have no connection
to Alabama other than my humanity

It's still impossible for me to see this
cute Americana street as anything other than a
KKK war zone, a siren-sounding boulevard,
a gaping wound whose stitches never took

Love Is the Loch Ness Monster

I've been hearing about the monster
since I was a kid

read about the beast in books
and heard stories from friends

even met a couple of guys who
claimed to have seen it

but they were filled with whiskey
so I'm not sure it counts

tales that span centuries

folklore galore

scientists, scholars, adventurers,
engineers, tourists, TV crews,
filmmakers, photographers, and
researchers

have all

taken a look

and come up empty

and the few that have gotten close
even caught a glimpse

have most likely been
swallowed whole

and gnashed

to bits

This Password

Sorry, your password does not contain one of the following:
Your password
must include a capital letter, two numbers,
an exclamation point, a decimal, an em dash
three ampersands, the initials of your
high-school crush, the code from
your first bike lock, a Van Halen reference,
a Shakespearean sonnet, a Biggie verse,
a symbol from the periodic table, the latitude of your
first kiss, the longitude of your last
one, an introspective look at Plato's
Apology, your driver's license number
divided by 12, Maya Angelou's birthday,
Rumi's favorite prime number, the amount of eggs
in your grandma's Bundt cake, the dollar amount
left by the tooth fairy for your first molar,
a Bible verse from Corinthians, the waist
size of your father's Lee's, your grandfather's
diastolic blood pressure, your heartrate when you lost
your virginity, your high score on Ms. Pac-Man, the
number of brooches owned by your mother,
the size of the first bra you unhooked, the highway
on which you received your first DUI, the amount
of times you've bought flowers in lieu of apologizing,
the postal address of the first house you egged,
the number of ingredients in your special BBQ rub
the horsepower of a '65 Thunderbird, the

number of pages in *White Fang,* the GPA of
that foreign-exchange student you cheated
off of in math class, the ring size of your
ex-wife, the day she began to feel unloved, the time of day
she called and said she wanted to meet at the park,
the sum of money her macchiato cost,
the time she took (in seconds) to tell
you she no longer loved you, the speed at which she
pulled away from the curb, the number of
times you've thought about her since

        Sorry, your password does not contain
            one of the following,
           please try again

        Sorry, that exceeds three attempts
          Please try again later

To the Little Girl with the Focused Smile Who
Blew Bubbles Out the Back Seat Window in Heavy
Traffic on the 405 Freeway—Full and Iridescent,
Some Solo, Others in Clusters, All of Them Delicate
and Bulbous, Traveling Amongst Masses of Metal,
Skirting Fenders and Grazing Hoods, Doing Their
Best to Steer Clear of Horsepower and Combustion:

                    Thank you

                            so much.

Where Serotonin Flows Like Saturated Fat
for Kate

I'm with you
and I'm happy
even on a Monday
even in Van Nuys
even with this blister
in my new Chuck Taylors

We are ordering
at Bill's Burger Shack
on Oxnard Street:
a double with cheese
for you, a single without
mayo for me

The old man, Bill,
conducts the griddle,
presses the beef down
with the back of his spatula,
allowing grease to hiss
and pop

And we sit at the counter,
and you sip your can of Coke
while we hold hands, when Bill
leans forward to tell me that it's
busy and that it'll be a while

And I nod and thank him,
because it's hard to think
of a more perfect sentence

In Summer

in summer
we rise early
& play late
under a sun
    that is eager to stay up, too

in summer
we get dirty
wear grass-stained knees
come home with mud on our clothes
    & trouble in our smiles

in summer
Chuck Taylor rubber thins
& swimsuits never have time to dry
& we dart through soft mounds of sprinklers
& eat watermelon smiles

in summer
we are boys
we are girls
we are animals

in summer
we are stars
    balls of energy
    & mass

burning from our cores
until deliciously tired

If You Must Know

you only hear about a tenth of my romantic thoughts
the rest would be too much of—what they call—a good thing
   like scarfing down hundreds of broccoli florets or putting
      down
crates of yams or popping penicillin like Bubble Yum
but recently, if you must know, afterwards, when we're in bed,
   lazing on pillows, the down comforter crinkling in our
      hands
my thoughts *do* swirl, and always land on familiar footing:
   giving up this 9-to-5 humdrum, hitting the open road with
      you, holing up
     in a one-bedroom outside of Omaha, sharing whiskey with
      rocks, and writing
        sweet nothings on your bathroom mirror that's covered
          with steam from your long showers

Obits

just once I'd like to see an honest obituary

tell me about someone who stress-ate donuts, who had a shitty temper
who dipped their pizza into ranch, and called people *fuck nuggets* on the 405

let me in on secrets, infidelities, credit-card fraud, abuse, drunkenness and darkness

stand at the pulpit and tell me about the devil, open the altar and the dead man's soul,
toss handfuls of dirt onto the casket
and onto the person

New Nikes

Your love is a new pair of
white Nikes
        which I'm trying to
        keep clean
        while hopping chain-link fences
        and riding New York City subway cars

The Wondrous Names of Roses

White, Red, Yellow, Pink, Mauve,

Iceberg, Valencia, Moonstone,
Gemini

Queen Elizabeth, Julia Child,
Black Magic, Hot Cocoa

Midas Touch, Betty Boop,
Glowing Peace, Hot Tamale

Knock Out, Cupcake,
Don Juan, Sexy Rexy

Gift of Life, Amber Queen,
Sun Sprinkles, Scentsational,

Applause, Gourmet Popcorn,
French Lace, Brass Band,
Starry Night, Baby Boomer,
Dream Weaver, Summer Wine,
Stairway to Heaven

This is the Day, Party Girl,
Daydream, Minnie Pearl,
Peaches 'n' Cream, Magic Carrousel,

Rise 'n' Shine, Gizmo,
Rockin' Robin, Rainbow's End

And, of course,
the lovely
Marilyn Monroe

i carry your heart with me by e.e. cummings
(without words)

   (
)   (
,   ;
,   )

   (,   )
   (,   )
,

   (;

)
           (   )

The Attic

Do you ever wonder what we look like in heaven?
Do we ascend and keep the age at which we expire?
Do we all become fifteen again?
Or thirty? Or forty-five?
Do we transform into when we were most happy?
Or do we all get the same face and body, a uniform
of sorts, so beauty as we know it becomes obsolete?
Or is heaven just similar to life here on Earth, but one
where we are gifted the acceptance of differences?
Is it just an attic, somewhere at 100,000 feet elevation,
where we finally spin around the sun in perfect harmony?

Permanent

Watching Mom get her hair done
for the first time
since I was a boy.

We're at a place on Magnolia St.,
a spot called
Curl Up & Dye.

Mom asked me
if she could get a permanent—
a new style—
following
her usual transfusion of
O positive,

so we found this salon
whose door was ajar
and whose Open sign
buzzed with neon.

The doctors told me her condition
is worsening,
that her time now
can be measured in months.

There's soft jazz,
the sigh of traffic on the main
road, and a fan that tickles
a pile of women's magazines
with each oscillation.

You like it? she asks.
She pats the sides.
She twists in the chair,
causing her sundress to get
an inch of lift.

Yes, I answer, as the hairdresser
continues to snip here and there.

I fixate on
Mom's gray curls
that flutter
to the bright linoleum,
knowing the broom will
soon come out, and that
those very follicles
will be pushed
by hard bristles
into a dustpan.

Jesus's Yelp Review of Panda Express

This is my first time using Yelp, so you'll have to pardon me if I'm not following the guidelines correctly.

I remember when the founder of Yelp, little Jeremy Stoppelman, was born. He was a sweet boy, a curious boy... always a bit of a snitch and gossip, but it's good to see that his vice became his vocation, and that his one-time weakness is now worth over 500 million.

Anywho, I'm here, in Venice, California, where a lot of you guys look like me, so I fit right in. Just want to grab a bite and try Panda Express. I know what you've done to pandas, so I was shocked (and relieved) to see they weren't on the menu. Hard to know with you humans. Part of me expected to see a bald-eagle-and-panda kebob as one of the combos.

The lady in front of me (her name's Betty Rega— and she's always been rude) asked to try the chicken and held the line up for three minutes, just chewing and *ooh-ing*. It's chicken, Betty. Come on. Use that imagination I gave you, and let's keep the line moving.

The Chow Mein's pretty good. It's about as Chinese as Andy Warhol (miss that little goober), but still packed with lots of flavor and shrimp and wondrous MSG. (Every time I give you guys a chemical, you seem to use them in your food. Hilarious.)

Traffic's rushing by on the main road, and I'm taking it in. You guys are buzzing about from lane to lane, honking and cursing, only minutes later to enter your homes, set down your bags, and kiss your children with those same mouths.

I have to be honest, I used to work harder with you all. I used to think that, at your cores, you were good. Sure, many of you—most of you—are just misguided. But I think I started mailing it in sometime around the internet's appearance. (I really just helped Gore invent that thing so that you guys could burn CDs.) But wow, did that backfire! Have you ever checked out the comments section on YouTube?—holy shit, right? I actually listened to some jazz the other day—a little Thelonious Monk—and wrote a comment about his unique sound and was told to "go get slapped by my own mama." Mary's not like that, though, and I didn't react right away, but rest assured that DolphinBaby42 will be receiving a jury duty summons in the coming weeks.

Yup, the comments section was it for me. I started showing up to the office a little later, playing a round of golf beforehand, and not even changing out of my spike cleats, just tracking in mud and sod across the clouds.

Then you all started with CrossFit. Hot damn! Enough already! I get it, I get it! You can lift a tire over your head. You still can't remember your wife's birthday or any of your children's ages, but I'll call you if I need a man who can shake some rope that's tied to a wall.

I still have hope, though. It's what I'm made of. Many of you are as sickened as I am. Many of you aren't sure how we got here. And that makes me keep at it. I need you more than you need me right now, if that makes sense. Don't make my heart melt as fast as those polar caps, okay?

I thought the Ten Commandments was a short enough list, but maybe it's too much reading for you folks.

So let's keep it simple and go back to that grammar-school golden rule. You remember that one, right? Good.

No, not *that* one. That's eye for an eye. And that was a *joke*.

Yes, that *other* one. About being good to each other. You *do* remember it?

Yes. Good. I thought you would. It was taught to you when you were a tiny tot, before you ingested all that trans-fat and your mind became as littered as Bourbon Street after Mardi Gras. Let's go back to that.

All right, kids, that was a little longer than I intended. Gonna go grab a drink cup and have a little orange Fanta . . . my salt level's higher than Mount Sinai.

Three stars.

Peace unto all.

Yours,

JC

Passing Tongues
Inspired by The Guardian article by Jo Tuckman and the piece by Uncle John

I.

The dying language is Kallawaya,
from South America,
Bolivia to be exact

high in the thin air
of the Andes

the Kallawaya people
see the benefits of compromise,

speaking Spanish to feign
peace with modernity,

yet, in private, the Kallawaya
use their own tongue,
only passed
in secret
by men

and while their skills as herbalists
and healers
are renowned throughout
the region

no salve nor
tree root can curb
their dwindling
their demise

time withering
the tribe
to now fewer
than one hundred

II.

Yuchi
is spoken by the
Yuchi people

originally from Tennessee
they were relocated
to dusty Oklahoma in the
late-1800s

forced to attend
government schools,
the Yuchi children
had to do without their
native roots

beaten whenever
comfortable speech
slid from their lips

the dialect
has ten genders,
including three for
inanimate objects

but only
five remaining
speakers

III.

Guugu Yimidhirr
a language
born and raised in
Queensland, Australia—

James Cook
encountered more than just
miles of sharp coasts
and rocky reefs
when he explored
Australia in 1770,

taking note of
a few words from the
Guuugu Yimidhirr,
the northern
Aboriginal people

the most famous
word scrawled in
Cook's journal is one
we still use today

kangaroo
though Cook spelled it
kangooroo

the tongue
is now spoken
by only two hundred
people

as it is continually
rejected in favor
of English

IV.

Tofa,
hails from Siberia,
the land
of stretching
tundra,
dark timber and
the world's deepest
lake

the language was developed
miles from the Artic
Circle as an efficient
way of communicating
complex reindeer-herding
directions

for example, condensing
*a male domesticated reindeer
in its third year and first
mating season, but not ready
for mating* to
just *döngür*

Tofa is now moribund

the young preferring
Russian

only thirty
people
still hold
Tofa's power

V.

Aka-Jera is
not taught in schools
or AP classes

its words distant from
Rosetta Stone programs
and SAT tests

just the oldest
continuously used language
on the planet

from the Andaman Islands,
in the Indian Ocean,
dating to the Neolithic Era,
around 8,000
years ago

these people
whose native tongue
decays with each day
live isolated,
two hundred miles
from the Asian mainland

their beats and inflections
of little relation to any
other

this once thriving culture,
now a tiny tribe
of only forty people

VI.

Nuumte Oote,
a language
from Mexico

where
a married couple
from the southern state
of Tabasco,
Manuel Segovia and
Isidro Velazquez,

are the only people
on the globe who
can utter the words
of a language that
literally means
true voice

the lone pair
to pass their voices
back and forth

everything
a code

everything
a secret

VII.

These languages
now ebb
like Amazonian
rainforests, red pandas,
and Cross River
gorillas

vowels, consonants,
diphthongs, and syllables

centuries of hellos,
good-byes, goodnights,
and I love yous

all last words

their rhythms and cadences

nothing more than
fluttering passenger pigeons

A Bistro & Baudelaire

On a gloomy day in both Celsius and Fahrenheit, the man sits down at a bistro, blocks from the Seine, while a drizzle pixilates the river, distorting the reflections of Gothic architecture. He scans the other patrons but only one catches his eye: a woman with deep expression lines who scrapes butter across her toast as a primer, then atop the butter, spreads a thick coat of black, seeded jam.

The drizzle strengthens into rain, causing some to open their umbrellas or scurry with a *Le Monde* draped over their heads. Others are used to Paris's mercurial moods, letting droplets collect in their hair and trace over their trench coats.

In time, the server brings the man an espresso. Sugar cubes arrive on a separate saucer, stacked like miniature bales of hay. The man pulls out the postcard he's purchased for his ex, feels the sharp corners and smooth surface. It's a banal card, a black-and-white shot of L'Arc de Triomphe, circa WWII. The address is a safe place to start, so he brings his pen to the horizontal lines and scrawls her name and street and *Massachusetts* and *USA* and *Air Mail/Par Avion*. He wipes his sweaty hands on his trousers, pictures her scarlet nails manipulating her P.O. Box lock, then imagines her soft fingers sorting through bills and junk and magazines, before meeting his card. Her

eyebrows will furrow, and she'll flip the card
to see his lazy penmanship. Will she go further?

A vendor along the bank of the river closes his
antique bookshop. In his cabinets are meaningful
words penned by de La Fontaine, Labé, Hugo, Pascal,
and Baudelaire. How many of those books, the man
wonders, would have been written without heartache?

The man requests a glass of cognac and it is delivered
promptly, served atop a glass of hot water to keep the
spirit warm. *Carla,* he writes. *Hi. I hope this finds you.
And I hope that it finds you well. I'm in Paris, should
you wish to find me. PS I wish my happiness wasn't
a memory.*

The man takes a good pull of his libation, listens
to the rain pelt the cobblestones, and reads over
his sentence. It isn't Baudelaire, he thinks,
but at least it's true.

Dear Jesus

It's me.
I'm not in church this time, but rather writing you a letter.
I figure you don't get much in the way of mail—except for Christmas lists—so maybe this note will make it to the top of your queue.
Why, I guess. That's all I want to know. Why?

If you could return to the space between BC and AD, year zero, I guess, and die for us again—would you? Why?

If you knew of the carnage and bloodshed that are indigenous to us humans, would you drag yourself down the same path, return to the hill of Golgotha, the cross on your back, dirt caked on your ankles, ribs nearly bursting through your emaciated frame? Why?

Were you God before you sacrificed yourself?
Were you more hopeful at 33 when you were more man than creator?

When you rose from the dead and the tomb was found empty, did you see life heading towards a more peaceful route? A loving one? A peace-be-with-you course? Does part of you wish you hadn't shifted the stone? Just left it there, sealing the entrance, with all that goodwill just wandering in your heart?

Do I dare ask if you were naïve?
Just young?

Or if you even hear us anymore?
Are you all out of mercy? Absolution?
Have we snapped your spirit like Eucharist wafers?

How's *your* faith?
Is this what you expected? The pain, pollution, selfishness, and harm?
What good is your Sunday body and blood if we just commit the same atrocities on Monday?

Are we all Judases?
All Pontius Pilates?
Have we all failed you?

How badly have we failed you?
Do we even want to know?
Will the knowledge do us any good?

Tired, but Beautifully So

it's exhausting work writing poems—
the coal mining of the brain—our
cerebrums cloaked in Dickies coveralls
and smeared with dirt

every day to unfurl an image
to the masses—take something
micro and make it macro, or vice
versa, and do so with cadence, and
song, and rhythm

to write something fresh but with
tradition—and reveal hope in the
hopeless, or tragedy in splendor

but my mind has been trained to
do this above all else

to never see a cloud as *just*
water vapor or a lavender field
as purple photosynthesis
or a child's tears as
solely sadness escaping
from eye ducts—

and that's okay,

I've accepted

it never has,

nor will it ever

A Giraffe's Heart

a giraffe's heart is the largest of any land animal,
at almost thirty pounds

(basically, the weight of a preschooler)

while the Etruscan pygmy shrew
has the smallest
of the mammal world

at 1.8 grams

(basically, a couple heavy pinches of salt)

and yet
        no matter
        the size,
        the shape,
        the blood pressure

        or beats
        per minute

the job of
any heart
is simple:

beat

until it can

beat

no
more

Mathieu Cailler is an award-winning author whose poetry and prose have been widely featured in numerous national and international publications, including the *Los Angeles Times* and *The Saturday Evening Post*. A graduate of the Vermont College of Fine Arts, he is the winner of a Short Story America Prize and a Shakespeare Award. He is the author of the short-story collection, *Loss Angeles* (Short Story America Press), which has been honored by the Hollywood, New York, London, Paris, Best Book, and International Book Awards; the poetry collection, *May I Have This Dance?* (About Editions), winner of the 2017 New England Book Festival Poetry Prize; and the children's book, *The (Underappreciated) Life of Humphrey Hawley* (About Editions), which has been nominated for the Caldecott Medal and the Newbery Award, among other notable prizes. *Catacombs of the Heart* is his second full-length poetry collection. Another children's book, *Hi, I'm Night*, is forthcoming from Olympia. For more information, please visit mathieucailler.com.

www.ingramcontent.com/pod-product-compliance
Lightning Source LLC
Chambersburg PA
CBHW022007120526
44592CB00034B/709